Apples & Stones

Apples & Stones

Poems by

Alice Wolf Gilborn

Cover design by Shay Culligan
Painting, "Baker Peak," by Mary Schwartz
www.mschwartzarts.com

ISBN: 978-1-952326-47-9

Kelsay Books
502 South 1040 East, A-119
American Fork, Utah, 84003

In memory of my grandmother, Alice Fisher Foster, who
taught me to use my imagination

Acknowledgments

I'm deeply indebted to James Crews for his insightful critique and help in selecting this collection of poems, and to their first readers: Northshire Poets Carol Cone, David Mook, Marcia Angermann, Peter Bradley, Monica Stillman, Brenda Nicholson, and Michelle Wiegers. Manchester Vermont's Northshire Bookstore has provided us with a space to meet and browse over the years; my sincere thanks to the Morrows. My husband Craig offers good comments when asked and observes silence when I write, for which I'm continually grateful. Finally, I wish to thank the editors of the journals and anthologies in which the following poems first appeared, a few in slightly different versions:

Bloodroot Literary Magazine: "Apples and Stones," "Learning Tai Chi," "Fireworks Before the Fourth"
Birchsong, v. II: "Berry Duet," "Dog Years"
Blueline Magazine: "The Pastoral"
Burlington Free Press: "Abandoned"
Healing the Divide: "End Results"
The Lyric: "Ninth Month"
The Mountain Troubadour: "Play by Play" (winner Gleason Memorial Award), "Endpath," "St. Francis"
Naugatuck River Review: "Salvage"
North Country: "Evening and Early Sorrow" (reprinted in *The Woman in the Mountain)*

Poems first published in my chapbook *Taking Root:* "Snow Script," "How to Fold an American Flag," "Catching It," "Don't Bite the Butterflies," "Not to Name the Hawk," "Leaning to the Light"

Contents

On the First Day of Spring

I seldom want to think about the past
now touched by death's inevitable eclipse,
ambition shadowed, love's moon clasped
by night, thoughts once open now a fist
in change's glove. Child no longer dreaming
of earth's springtime renewal, pleasured
bees in applebloom, sparrows preening
by a puddle, all my fool's gold treasure
hidden. Yet like the mist dissolving sun
that spreads its light across the mountain,
wonder breaks on me unbidden and once
again I'm young and time's a starry fountain,
droplets silver and unceasing, for the holding.
Too soon the clouds drift in, too soon enfolding.

Snow Script

Early March and cold
but the long light of
afternoon means spring
is near. Still, I am reluctant
to close this book on winter,
on the notes scrawled across
its white pages.
There, in the morning
when I make my narrow
way through the woods,
I see the hieroglyphics
of birds and the tiny tread
of a vole documenting
its long journey between
holes. Rabbits and squirrels
leave soft tripods;
wild turkeys make contact
in a jumble of three-
pronged forks.
When I am first
to break the snow, deer will
sometimes follow, poking
their pointed hoofs through
my broad tracks. You don't
have to be a hunter
to read the snow.

Once on a ski slope
while I dangled overhead
on the lift, I spotted
the tracks of a fox,
its catlike prints
a precise line of cloverleafs
in the snow, and a few
yards later the lovely, looping
signatures of many foxes
that had convened at some
moonlight rendezvous.

I rarely see this nighttime
traffic, the deer or the
foxes or the turkeys, all
the nocturnal busyness
of woodland animals
trying to feed, to find
shelter, survive—who,
unlike me, are innocent
of the text they write.
And sometimes
when I try to walk
the path the deer and I
have made, I can't; melted
snow has frozen into potholes
and I stumble forward,
sliding off the track
or sinking deep,
messing up the story,
never quite able to follow
precisely in another's
footsteps.

Leaving the Ocean

—for Penny

Leaving the ocean I carry it with me
breakers that stain the sand like flames

shadow ships on the horizon, a pelican's plunge
for shadow fish. Skin prickly with salt, March light

silver on water always moving, low roar of sea
slapping shore, sucking earth. Above it, our laughter.

Northbound, I'm the pelican's dive from sun to shade
color to black and white, landscape withdrawing

to a former season. Trees losing leaves, buds closing,
earth patched with old snow, sea breeze a cold wind,

whatever we had to say receding. When at last spring
breaks, slides its green shadow up New England's coast

in first flower of morning I know what I left is pure
memory, composed of all the oceans I've seen, times

I've stood with you on a beach looking seaward. A bright
and soundless picture, not real at all but far more true.

Abandoned

Take an old walk and see a new thing.
Look where the trail doesn't go

up the mountain stripped by winter,
oak and pine in supplication

to a crystalline sky. Animal tracks,
yesterday's half-covered on this verge

between settled and wild, don't count.
You almost pass it—years unnoticed,

the neglected boat in its tumbledown shed

docked at the edge of a snowfield lake,
ready to ply across, leaving time in its wake.

Hollyhocks

have taken their sweet
spring time to climb
the wall to the window
sill, stalks tipped with buds
heavy as marbles, and now
they bloom, opening their
pink satellite dishes
to receive a host of bees
broadcasting summer.

Mornings through
the window I look for
fresh flowers knowing
that many beneath the sill
have already spent their
lives, faded cones littering
the ground, and soon 9-foot
stems, leaves like platters will
be what's left of seasonal
extravagance, here and gone
with the bees. Yet roots
I cannot see foretell
a certain future.

Leaning to the Light

Our neighbor planted twelve
bulbs in the shadow of his barn
in the shadow of the trees
in the shadow of a mountain.
And now a dozen lilies grow
at an angle toward the sun
that touches them only
in the afternoon. Our neighbor
sold his house to part-timers
who come just for a week
or two so they never see
their flowers bloom, later
than the rest, their soft pink
petals tinged with white,
curled like shavings, stamen-
like antennae tuned to the western
sky. Like me, since I left the land
where I was born, leaning west,
these laggard lilies with mouths wide
open drinking in the setting sun.

Salvage

Surely the priest must have blessed it
as it rose gleaming from those soft
New England woods, the young Father
and his new church, house of God.

Timbers of spruce, roof of slate, fruits
of forest and mountain, it stood clean
in the sunlight, while within stirred the
breath of creation, whisper of God.

It held steady over the years, ripened
as its people claimed it for their own,
sheltered some, inspired others,
comforted the hopeless, touched by God.

Then the people scattered, their church
became irrelevant and the priest no
longer served. Vines crept across closed
doors, grass grew between the steps.

When yellow tape and the sign—
"Deconstruction Works"—appeared in front,
we knew its spirit had finally fled, an empty
house whose light now fell through the open

roof like rain. Yet the walls and wooden
arches with their crude quatrefoil designs still
stood as wind stirred the trees between its ribs,
a beached vessel long abandoned.

Perhaps it was more provident to take it
down than to let it rot in the woods. The
boards were worth something. Slates
unbroken could be reclaimed.

But what dignity in absence, in empty
space? Behind it stretched the graveyard,
its dead still needing it. Even a crumbling
frame can hold the cup of veneration.

Better to let it be, let saplings overgrow
and bless it, let its grave be the forest from
which it rose, the forest that will surely
swallow it, timber by timber, earth to earth.

Apples and Stones

When the river spills from its banks,
rushes down the road, it brings us gifts
from its heart—sand and rocks
and something else—

apples—shaken from laden trees,
hundreds of them, so when the water
withdraws it leaves a line of apples and stones
across all the yards on the street.

We flee from the muddy current as we
would from a snake's tongue licking
the fence lines, the grass, the arborvitae.
We return to pools and rivulets in the fields,
water in the cellar two feet deep.

The day after the flood, power is out
and people are out on the street—the fire
truck pumps basements, others dump
dirt on washed out driveways, pick up
begins. We compare damages.

Later the excavator crawls up the road
to the spot where the river boiled over,
shoves the channel back to its bed. The way
over the mountain is strewn with boulders.
But we can cross a bridge to town, leave our
mud flats, yesterday's gardens. We can stay.

Butterflies sip from sagging roses.
Claudia next door brings us a hibiscus cutting
from a bush in her yard, a pink tissuey flower
that lasts a day. *Put it in water and it will grow
roots,* she says. She tosses her apples into the field
for the deer. Ours just disappear.

Months later we wear an apron of sand
and stones on our grass, not as a badge
of courage or to show that we've suffered,
but as a mark of respect—
for change that lurks in every dry bed
for the fact that we can be routed again
for the truth that rivers will have their way.

St. Francis

arrived when the beaver dam upstream
broke in a wild rush of muddy water that roiled
our placid brook, breached the culvert, swept across
the road and pooled on our neighbor's lawn.

We found him on his back jammed against a rock—
feet, one arm broken, the other extended but no
hand. For two days he rested in the ebbing water
until we sought to rescue him, a small damaged

statue now standing beside our winter garden,
his head just above the snow. Ragged, useless,
we might have thrown him out. Yet we took
delight in this humble gift from someone's

yard upstream. Perhaps his outstretched arm
channeled a blessing; for water spared our cellar,
filled grass with loam where flowers later bloomed
then settled in its bed like a lion in the sun.

Boundaries

We live in a village that thinks
it's a farm. In the fluid margin

between town and country, we
go about quotidian tasks, tend

the garden, mow the grass
in the shade of old maples while

two blocks over a siren howls
in pursuit down the highway,

a truck dumps gravel at the town
garage. On that same street live

two goats and six handsome hens
picking ticks in their owner's yard,

potential fox bait. Behind us a pen
with horses and a donkey whose

foghorn bray is echoed by a blast
from the train parked across the road

from the Jiffy Store while its driver
gets his lunch. *Keep those animals*

out, some grumble, *they don't belong.*
Build a fence, pass a law, we pay

taxes to live in a town, not a barn.
But whose land is it? Have we

forgotten our heritage, a great northern
forest once visited, not owned? A blue

heron stands in the brook bisecting
our lone acre; deer browse beside it.

When the bear destroys the feeder
we don't shoot him. If the ground

hog prefers our lawn to the field
next door where he keeps his den,

we let him be. So he eats the tulips—
we'll plant more, not a fence.

How to Fold an American Flag

For twenty-three years
it rested on the fireplace
mantel, a neat triangle
fading in the Colorado
sun beneath the narrow
stained glass window.
We saw it but forgot,
even my mother
who accepted it that
cold November day in
1987 from the dutiful
honor guard at the
military cemetery, a
ceremony my father
must have witnessed
hundreds of times.
I did not attend his
funeral two thousand
miles away. But I heard
the shots in my bones,
for my father
this time, a salute
to the West Pointer,
pilot, bird colonel,
base commander.
For World War Two.
Son of a Lutheran
minister, he traded
church for country.
Faith, loyalty, patriotism—
inseparable.

After my mother died,
the old house sold,
my father's flag came
to me. It arrived in
a mid-sized priority
mailbox, featherlight.
We would buy a pole
for it, hang it for
Memorial Day. When
we unfolded it, three
empty shells fell out.
It was as bright as if
newly minted, except
where the sun had
tapped it. Large enough
to cover a coffin.

For three days in May
it hung like a quilt
from the porch rafters,
pinned up at the bottom
not to touch the ground.
That weekend I thought
about my father, about
all the questions I never
asked him, the love
I never showed him,
the life I never knew
about. On Tuesday
we unpinned the flag,
stretched it flat, folded it
according to instructions
found on the Web,

stripes over stars twice
blue field on the outside,
three triangles until only
the faded stars showed.

Catching It

The bee is a brown buzz
in the trumpet of the flower
and I hover, about to clamp
it with a cup, convey it by
sleight of hand to the Mason jar.
Bees already caught sticky
foot it up the sides, hang
from the lid, clear wings folded.
Don't bring that bottle in the house
warns my mother. But I do,
hiding it in my blouse, making
a bee line for my room.

I am tripped, tricked, can't blame
my brother he is nowhere in sight.
Shattered glass covers the floor;
air vibrates with bee fury
and I am leaning over the stair
rail crying, collection lost
consequences to pay. Then a
burning dart under my skirt
and another and I shriek. As if
by magic, my father swarms
up the stairs, hand raised.

Stung.

Mother Load

Out my window
through the bare trees I
can see the horses, woolly
and undefined, just beyond
the fence that separates our
house from our neighbor's.
One dark shape moves toward
something; three more are at
its heels. I see what they're after,
a person, a woman I think, pulling
a sled piled with hay which she
throws in little heaps on the snow.
A skirmish, a horse kicks, another
ducks its tail and bucks, then all
settle down to eat.

I am a girl again, watching
through my bedroom window
my mother, a small figure in shorts
and galoshes, as she crosses the field below
toting a shovel. Periodically she stops,
jabs it in the ground, uploads a chunk
of mud, then continues to make her way
along the small ditch that bisects the back
pasture. She says she likes irrigating,
but I don't. I'm glad to be in my room,
not out in a wet field, building little dirt
dams in the ditch, eyes peeled for snakes.
I'm draft dodging; she hasn't found me yet.
But I still feel guilty for not helping,
though I'm certain she'll tell me I'm
doing it wrong—I don't know how
to get a decent head, still haven't
learned where the water wants to go.

Now, I rationalize, I would have
been intruding. She had her thoughts,
content to be alone with them as long
as she kept moving. She may have been
thinking of the thirsty grass under her feet
or the good deal she got on that young
mustang mare. She liked to bill herself
as a horse trader, never a housewife.
She would not have been thinking of
cooking dinner or of me, daughter
recalcitrant. This was her time
for reflection under the bruising
Colorado sun as water fanned across
the field and snaked in bright rivulets
through the grass that would revive
overnight then grow and grow until
there was enough and more to feed
all her hungry horses.

Crystal Cuts

It's been years since I had one
even the thought of one, sweet,
tangy, you could suck on it
for an hour, each Crystal Cut
the epitome of sticky perfection.

They came in a white box
presented to me by my grand-
mother when I'd been a good
girl—cherry, lime, orange, lemon—
each in its own little package
of cellophane sparkling
on a bed of snowy tissue.

Oh, they were beautiful
those Crystal Cuts, strangely
translucent, jewels catching
the light, each the size of
a cork and hard as a rock.
I wanted to save them, savor
them, admire them at will;
more, I wanted to eat them—
and I did, thinking ahead to
the lemon even as the last of
the cherry drizzled down my throat.

I knew when Nana enlisted
my mother to drive her to
downtown Denver that her sweet
tooth was acting up; soon she
would be lunching with her
powdery friends on chicken

salad and finger rolls at Bauer's,
a candy shop to rival Schrafft's
of New York, though Denver
was hardly a metropolis yet.
She would return with an ample
supply of chocolate bonbons
and maybe, if I was deserving,
Crystal Cuts for me.

The whole time she was gone
I pondered my recent commissions
and omissions. The moment she
alighted from my mother's truck,
her default mode of transport,
I looked for a white box.
Nana almost always had one
but made me wait for it,
as if waiting for indulgence
was the only way to build
character in the young. Now,
after all these years, I thank her.

Learning Tai Chi

Practice one hundred
hours until the muscles
remember, one thousand
hours until you learn it
says the master.
This, the first of one
hundred eight positions
in one routine, Yang's
long form *Taijiquan.*

I will be dead.

So why do I come week
after week to this class
in the children's room
at the local bookstore
to stare at the spines
of *Goodnight Moon*
and *Pat the Bunny*
when I should focus
only on *ward off left,
ward off right* and the
106 steps that follow?
I'll be lucky to learn
even the beginning
of *grasp swallow's tail.*

Now I turn on my heel,
on my toe, shift
from leg to leg, full,
empty, but what happened
to my arms drifting in a

vague semaphore above
my head, where do they
belong? Where do I,
dodger of conflict,
fit in this slow dance
of martial art?

*Single whip, white crane
spreads wings*—metaphors
from ancient China
ghost the room as my
teacher in white
flows from step to step
his strength and easy grace
the discipline of years.

Against all reason
I imagine I can do this
dance, as well as
a thousand things I imagine
I can't. Reason is a rock,
imagination a river.
A child again in a children's
room—*embrace the tiger,
repulse the monkey,* yin,
yang, *high pat on horse*—
I move to the music of
all things possible.

Open Heart

My son lost his heart three times: to
the mountains he loved, to the woman
he married, and lately, to the puppy
he brought home from Colorado.

But it was the other time, the real
time, that sends a shiver down my
spine on this hot August afternoon
almost a year to the day when he

lay supine in that bright, sterile
room, the instruments that would
soon invade his body lined neatly
on a table—knives, forceps, saw—

the masked and gloved doctors
who would use them to pry his chest
apart, cut to the bone. They took his
heart from him, held it in their hands

hooked it up, and all that day I could
hear in my mind's distance the beep,
beep, beep of the machine that nourished
it. *Please,* I cried to no god at all. *Please.*

And then they put it back, quivering.
Restored, we celebrated, thanked
surgeons, technology, our lucky day.
But knowing now how easy it is to lose
your heart, I pray. *Please. Oh please.*

Tenacity

At the nursery's fall sale he has
bought himself a rosebush whose
buds promise pink blossoms,
but he reads that the bush is for
a milder zone. Never mind, he'll
put it in the cellar to winter over
and plant it in the spring.

The way to grow roses in a cold climate,
he insists.

She has ordered a new desk
calendar, though her prognosis
doesn't look good, and she's
already filling it up with meetings
and appointments, not medical,
mind you, but essential to her
tenure at the library.

A professional lives for her work,
she lets you know.

Dog and cat materialize
in the kitchen prompted by
internal clocks—they wait
by their bowls, eyes on owner,
who mindlessly goes about her
business stuffing a chicken.

If they sit and stare long enough,
someone will feed them.

Call it tenacity or blind faith
that lets us suppose the rose
will bloom, the meeting will occur,
the bowl will be filled. That lets me
think I can balance my checkbook
or write the next great poem;
that disaster will elude me
and the sun will also rise.

Play by Play

"He *skys* the ball to right field," sings the radio.
Will the ball then *earth* in the fielder's mitt?

Can you *sea* a ship or *mountain* a bike?
Bike a mountain, yes, but don't ship a sea.

Consider the sun—how skyed, it drops
behind the mountain, how it's caught

by the sea, how it slips to the other side
of earth, rises, arches, skyed again….

Someone in Japan skys a ball to left field
while here in the dark the radio prattles on.

If I Had the Time

If I had the time I'd learn the robin's song
And whistle it at dawn.

If I had the time I'd ride a rocky mountain
And bridle my past.

If I had the time, I'd moonwalk in a forest
And capture my fear.

If I had the time, I'd kneel in a churchyard
And ground my unbelief.

If I had the time, I'd build a grassy bower
Lined with bones and feathers and shiny stones,

And if I had the time, I'd stretch in the sun
And wait for you to enter hour by hour.

End Results

His turn for blood work this morning.
A routine test, but no breakfast, not
even coffee. Just twelve degrees—
I offer to walk the dog, and after
the long ritual of dressing for frigid
weather, I plunge into the heartless air.
An orange cat crouched in the driveway
shifts its front paws; puffed up jays
squawk in the oak tree. The dog
stops—then sneezes mightily,
putting cat and cold on notice.

When I get back, he's settled in his
favorite chair, newspaper on his lap.
Table's set for one; a pot of water
boiling on the stove awaits its egg,
tea bag sits in a mug, a single slice
of toast is ready to pop. The radio
is off for once, so it's our own voices
we hear, chatter we won't remember
in a room warming with winter sun.
When he leaves, silence descends
like yesterday's snow.

Eating my solitary breakfast,
I think of his small habitual gestures,
the way he has of wanting to nourish
the living: sparrows peck seed he's
spread on the deck, his two feral
cats feed at their bowl, at the table

I'm about to crack a perfect egg.
Sustenance of many years. I wish
him well, I wish him love, food
for our braided lives. I wish
all results positive.

Someone Has to Drive

He is driving and I am watching, not
the road for traffic or for deer but mountains

hunkered on this autumn morning like great calico
cats wearing a pastiche of hardwoods, softwoods

morphed from summer's verdant tedium into
a new palette—maples gone red, oaks shimmering

like bronze coins, cones of golden tamaracks
threading the marsh, all patterned by light

and shade, gray replacing blue in a restless sky.

Look, look at the mountains, look at those clouds!
I cry, forgetting that someone has to drive.

I scramble to find words for fall's evolving
scene writing them down fast on the back of my

market list but he is occupied, eyes straight ahead
constant as the ever green of pine as he recites

the price of gas at every service station, counts
aloud the UPS trucks passing in a long brown line.

Berry Duet

Fifty-nine years and we never sang together
but now on either side of the big blueberry

bush, where we've assigned each other
picking spots—he gets the high berries

I, the low. We begin our ageless argument
"Anything you can do I can do better"

high and low, off and on, as berries, blue
soft, too soft drop into our baskets. Off key

we're singing still, together. And later on
the radio, Beethoven's "Ode to Joy," while

we listen in silence, throats catching at
the sheer beauty of it, then and now.

The Pastoral

I've heard it so many times
it doesn't surprise me anymore

though I anticipate the part
where the sky begins to clear

after the storm. Beethoven,
master of symphonic storms,

has hinted at this melody
all along, but now on this sun

lit day in April I am pierced anew
by the aptness, the grandeur of it.

Not surprising after such a bleak
week, disappointment, anxiety,

boredom, the hospital run as
efficiently as a container ship

sailing uncertain seas, its cargo
balanced between life and death.

I sit by his side for hours in the
pre-op cubical, then alone for hours

in the post-op lounge with its stuffed
chairs, free coffee and muted TV.

We drive home in the snow, the sixth
day of it, flakes drifting like flowers.

At last on this sun blessed morning,
radio on, we watch the stream slide

through our yard, the only movement,
even the squirrels are still, not a flutter

in the trees whose long shadows splay
across the winterblown earth. I think

of nothing but the music as the fifth
movement starts with a few delicate

notes then begins to swell, calm
after storm, but nothing is tranquil

about this airy melody as beneath
it a faint syncopation stirs and rises

until in that blossoming of sound
I feel the balance tilt toward life.

McFerren Wedding

reads the handmade sign posted on
the red barn by the side of the road

where it's hung for years, something
we see and don't see as we drive past,

like a marker commemorating some
battle or statesman or bridge, names

forgotten but persistent in their anonymity.
Today, for some reason, I wonder how

the McFerrens are doing, not that I've
ever met them, neither Mr. McFerren

whose name is on the sign, nor the name-
less bride he married. After the earnest

vows and nervous toasts, that barn must
have rocked on their wedding night, music

dancing, the somber mountains nodding
above in silent approval. Is it safe to say

the two have kept their pledge, made a home
made multiple McFerrens as expected?

In the wake of winter the barn's roof sags
like a sway backed horse, sign askew but firm.

Could it have been the scent of those white
blossoms this morning on the little magnolia

tree in the yard next door, the first bulletin
of spring after long dark and frozen earth

that made me see again the weathered promise
nailed to this red barn by the side of the road?

Ninth Month

—for Amanda

I wish I could sleep on my stomach
I'm tired of my side and my back
My hair stands up straight
As if combed by a rake
And my neck has developed a crack.

Once I could dream on my stomach
Sail off in a hot air balloon
Now the baby within
Has no room to swim and has
Grown as full as the moon.

If I could just sleep on my stomach
I'd go early to bed, not late
But my stomach's a hummock
With a very high summit
So back on my back is my fate.

Mother's Day

The whistle of the train
bounces off the mountains
that first sharp blast at my back
sudden, repeated, stone in still water
rippling outward ever diminished
until even the echo is gone.

It reminds me of my children,
the intensity of their young lives,
the pitch of their urgent demands
that drops, dissolves slowly into
an inconceivable future, leaving
me standing here, still, in time.

Spaces

It took a week to move the trailer.
First they stripped its underpinning letting
wires and insulation dangle like a ragged
bedskirt. Then the people living there moved
out, took their dogs, left their house; silence
filled the space.

When I walked up the street
for a look, a neighbor gave me peaches
from her tree, lobbing the rotten ones over
the stone wall toward the trailer shell. *Need
to clear off my ground so fungus don't spread,*
she told me.

This morning the cab of a semi
backed in, hitched up the trailer, and in minutes
the completed truck had clipped down the road
out of sight. Now an empty rectangle of dirt
bounded by rocks and flowers—and peaches.

With time and new grass it might be
a pocket park, I muse, while I watch a crow flap
its way across the face of a cloud, a black speck
on immense white.

The Crazy Lady

one street over didn't get any mail
today and neither did I. She had
a hand in her box when I drove by
(careful not to smile or wave)

then pulled back without a thing,
stared at me a moment, threw open
her arms. In my own box, nothing but
an ad from a used car dealership.

In the absence of mail I considered
the look she gave me. Why do I call
her crazy—because she hums too loudly
to herself in the Rite Aid, or because

her ancient Ford Escort, back end tied up
by tape and bungee cords, haunts all
the parts of town I frequent? Maybe she's
just too close for comfort when she stops

in the middle of the road to roll down her
window and start a conversation with me,
a perfect stranger. I don't want her stories.
Her invitation to intimacy makes me hurry on.

Yet her glance, the way she spread her arms
wide in a bleak embrace of emptiness,
makes me wonder—have I been using
the wrong word for loneliness?

Evening and Early Sorrow

—for Sally

Always when I look at you
I see the shadow of your son
upon your face. Eyes dark
as moth's wings, his smile
a sudden bend of light.
Turned ten you let him
ride his birthday with your
friend in that bright, swift
hunkered-down machine
pressing the mountain road
until the missed curve seemed
like flight, the car a comet
looping through the trees.

Later you knew. Sirens
you never heard shattered
your skull, flames gutted
your heart. Yet you stand
here, black eyes circling my
own boy with his big hands,
pants an inch above his ankles
wanting out, wanting to go
if only for an hour. There
is nothing we can save him
from. He runs toward the sun
while we wait, bracketed
by ghosts, in the slow dusk
of his leaving.

Blue Madonna

Passing through the village
the train plays a plaintive tune

on this January day. I wonder
if the little blue Madonna

in the woods by the abandoned
church hears it—should I tell

her what it is? But she's as silent
as the snow she blesses, lost
in a wilderness of hemlocks.

Kate's Window

It's cancer she said as casually as she might
have said it's Tuesday, you're all invited.

And indeed it was a Tuesday when she held
her little party six months later, when she

threw open the door with a smile and throaty
laugh, her head totally bald. She must have

cried the night she heard the news about her
biopsy, but she never mentioned despair

though she wasn't one to hold back the chaos
in her life—her estranged husband, doctor,

womanizer, her children, all three who
struggled with addiction—she willingly

supplied graphic details. In therapy when
I first met her, she remained for all the years

I knew her. I think perhaps she welcomed
something definite, even the news of her

death. I helped her put together a booklet
of her poems, *Kate's Window*; we both knew

it was for her friends as much as for herself.
At her service I read the one about the elms

in Autumn, stripped of leaves, still beautiful.
Her photo of a vase of bright flowers in a multi-

paned window, leaves quilting the forest floor
outside, trees receding to an unknown distance,

now hangs on my bedroom wall next to my own
window. You'd like it there, Kate. I hope it's

Tuesday where you are, and you're planning
a party—just for friends.

Please

Give me the calm
of the sleeping dove
as I watch the river rise.

The silence
of the stalking cat
when angry voices clash.

The prudence
of the nursing mare
whose greedy foal insists.

The vision
of the toddling child
who reinvents the world.

Give me the courage
to free what I'm unfit to care for,
to keep only what I have to give.

Endpath

This avenue of moving ants is not a street
in Manhattan, nor the five o'clock crawl
of traffic on the George Washington Bridge,
but a highway they have carved in the grass
from the edge where the weeds begin
to an unseen city beneath our deck.

Some are on their way to the office;
others, large and sleek, have an audience
with the queen; still others have fallen
into a manhole, one of many in their road.
A work crew, carpenter ants, is busy building
a side street leading to the crabapple tree.

Today I know of two weddings, people I
don't know, so I won't be going. Still, I wish
them perfect weather, blue sky, puff clouds
no wind. I wish them purpose in their train
of days, that their children follow graciously;
and if their path leads to the queen, they take
the other one, to the tree. And get to know it.

Deer Night

Deer have ghosted the white field
leaving tracks like split almonds;
they have pawed the snow

under the crabapple tree
nibbled the frozen pumpkin,
remnant of Halloween.

I watch for them tonight
when the moon has made them
bold, its light as cold as snow.

I wait for them to show me
their secret lives like a door
that opens when you pass by

but sleep shuts my eyes.
They are safe.

Chimera

Milkweed flares yellow
in green fields, on lawns
a flush of political signs.

Sound and fury reigns
throughout the land.

Elections should be held
in spring, when hope is
just around the corner.

Now, in Indian summer,
arguments kindle, derision
flames like dying leaves.

In these warm days
how eager we are to praise

the illusion that suits us,
forgetting kindness, forgetting
the season that follows.

Don't Bite the Butterflies

We take it every day
the dog and I
this path connecting
field and woods
unruly verge of blooms
invaded by insects.
On course we march
with details of butterflies—
swallowtails swoop
fritillaries flit
checkerspots skip
and those little ones,
the forest's punctuation—
commas and question
marks—dash. Admirals
convene on the grass.
We have our rules
the dog and I—flick flies
knick gnats, bat bees—but
don't bite the butterflies.
One commands a hill
of dung, gift of the dog.
Slowly it fans its black
wings banded with white
a semaphore repeated
perfectly by its comrades
in the field.

To My Dog Under the Bed During a
Thunderstorm

You could teach a course in it.
Explosions 101: Firecrackers,
Gunshots, Thunder Claps.
Canine Mindless Panic,
Feline Blind Indifference.
The tags on your collar chatter,
eyes roll with the thunder
though I can't see you in your
den amidst the dustballs. You've
forgotten yesterday's storm and all
the others when you emerged intact.

If I told you that the sound won't hurt
I'd be lying—you've sensed its deadliness.
Lightning's a serpent's tongue—
only this snake can't be caught, tossed
in the air until its back is broken. Being
human we know the consequence
of terror. But the fear of what we don't
know, what we imagine and you can't,
is a fear that snaps the spirit.
When the sun breaks out you'll
crawl from under your darkness,
and I'll keep listening as I do
each day for distant thunder and watch
the strange indifferent clouds
glide slowly toward me.

Dog Years

Neither of us wants to climb the hill
at the end of the road.
I go ahead, tugging on the leash
because I know the climb
will do me good as it should the dog.
Coming down she takes the lead;
I wonder when her brisk trot became
a walk. We pussyfoot home,
virtuous on rickety legs.

The time that has bound us, animal
and human, has put us on
parallel tracks like skiers, dog lagging
behind in her puppy days,
sliding up to me in middle years
then slipping past, catching
me by surprise. I don't want to witness
her cataracts, her deafness,
her existential whining at her contracted
world. Slow failures I compare
with mine. Only her nose excels.

This morning she caught the ball
I threw for her, chased the cat,
sniffed the snow, barked at the dogs
next door. We took our time—
playing, welcoming daylight,
going for a walk; tomorrow we'll
do the same. She won't remember
the hill. The difference is, I will.

Puppy Bound

Maybe I shouldn't have saved the ad
for a year or torn the new one from the
paper or asked the breeder to send pictures
of the seven live mops she sought to sell.

Maybe we should have left the carrier
at home before we drove south to have
a look, saying we had to think about it,
a small puppy was a big commitment.

Now we are penned, rooms barricaded,
baby gates at the stairs, lamps unplugged,
shoes elevated. Bonded and bound. We knew
the price of love would mean imprisonment.

So why did common sense take a nap
the day we brought her home?

Hospice

I've watched the cat
all week hold dear
to his life, like watching
a climber dangling
from a rockface, hands
sliding down the rope
one notch at a time
until finally he lets go,
falling into space.

Seventeen years
with this cat; it's
time. But it's not.
I should trust him to
the mercy of the vet
stop trying to divine
his animal quotient
of pain. I feed him baby
food by the teaspoon
carry him from couch
to chair, pillow of
bones. I keep him
here, I know, because
of my own pain, because
I didn't let my mother
age at home, because
I believe I know
what this cat wants,
but I don't.

Not to Name the Hawk

When you see a hawk, the story goes,
it's a message from a loved one. A week
before my brother died a young hawk, a
failed hunter, landed on the feeder—
I could hear the rush of wings as small
birds scattered. It was so close I could
have touched it but for the pane
of glass between us. For a time
we stared at each other while
I studied the streaks on its
breast hoping to name
and place it. I hadn't
heard the story yet.

If it carried
a message I think
I know what it was as
surely as the small birds
knew. And the loved one who
sent it—there are many. But to
believe in signs is to suffer
Cassandra's fate. Did Jesus come
first as a hawk and no one told of
it? Did he do any better as a man?
It is safer not to know the future,
not to name the hawk, not to believe
that it itself is the message it carries.

Turkey Season

Every year it surprises us
though we've been waiting
for it, wanting it—snow
rotten beneath our feet,
mud, then crocuses, robins,
blackbirds reclaiming
earth and air. Cardinals
grow insistent, goldfinches
brightly metamorphose
while dandelions conquer
the fields. The bush we thought
winterkilled has sprouted buds,
ragged trees along the back
road stand in full dress, their
white perfume worth the walk.

Yesterday the orioles arrived
twelve months to the day
they appeared last year,
oblivious to our timetable,
drawn north by temperature
and light—territorial, brilliant,
hardwired to defend domains.
If they had not shown up, we
would have been surprised, or
worried, since we've adapted
our strategies to theirs.

Then, at daybreak, a rifle
cracked once, silencing
birdsong, while anger pooled
in my chest at being awakened,
at being reminded of death
when life was just returning.

Dove of the Morning

I believe I remember you
every place I've lived

your gentle call, the whistle
of your wings in flight

bird of my Colorado childhood
who heralded morning light

more so than the fenced rooster
who crowed at any time of day.

West, east here in Vermont,
common everywhere I'm told,

a little flock lined up at dawn
on the limb of a dead butter

nut tree, some roosting
underneath, hunkered down

like chickens, until all erupt
as one upon the vibrant air.

Days are grayer at this place in my
life, whatever I wanted so much

I'm forgetting, whomever I loved
so much will be gone. Still, your

continuity comforts me. Dove
of my mornings, you've called

to me these many years—When will I
know to call you by your real name?

The Great Blue

heron steps down the middle of a thin stream
that threads our property, sword beak sheathed
on his breast. It's December, no frogs, no fish. Yet

he persists, raising one stick leg after the other in
a slow dance, toes grasping icy stones until he
reaches the culvert. I wonder if he'll try to follow

the stream under the road but instead he hops to
the shoulder, neck extended, small head turning
this way and that. Slowly he spreads his heavy

wings, lifts off, lands with a thud on the other side
then pauses to gather his feathered self together.
Cautiously he resumes his watery walk.

He was right to fly over the road, not cross on foot.
Instinct must have told him it could be a ribbon
of death for creatures unaware. Or maybe it was

the dark smell of asphalt, this broad leaden swath
dividing land and water, alien to a creature whose
element is air. His choice was easy.

The Whitethroat Sings

Voices of children at play and birdsong
mingle on this second day in May,
birthday of our son. Though I want
to celebrate it on the twelfth, when
we brought him home, an infant
stranger who changed our lives.

I sometimes wonder about his first ten
days, the mother, father, parents he
never knew. From that morning when
first we held him, he became our child
our teacher, a gift unknown, unfolding
like the yellow tulip my spouse has
placed in the bud vase in the window.

This morning I hear the whitethroat sparrow
sing its high galloping notes for the first
time this spring. Trees reach skywards
in nets of budding leaves, grass still too
tender to hold my steps, but clouds hold
back their rain. The day is laced with
green and gray. Among birds crowding
the feeder, I see my sparrow, here all along.
So much life.

Littleton

—in memory of Columbine

All week the wind pushes from the west
pushing bands of waves across the lake
pushing them toward shore, lap after
lap, riffling the feathery
hemlock, the male mallard
bobbing on the water, solitary,
hen brooding in the woods somewhere
hour after hour, riding the little
waves until finally he climbs to shore
and turns facing them, not hoping,
not grieving, waiting. It is
April and the wind is cold.

When I think of Littleton, I think
of landscapes. Of fabled country,
scrub oak, cactus, gullies—of Joseph
Bowles, buffalo hunter, gold miner,
riding down from Central City
rope and rifle on his saddle all the way
from river to foothills claiming everything
in between. Colorado territory. Bowles knew
how much dry land it took to graze cattle.
His barbed wire was the best.

Of the country I grew up in, sectioned
off for farms, cottonwoods shading
irrigation ditches, alfalfa, sugar
beets in the bottom land, Littleton's
giant grain mill on the Platte grinding
all day, ton upon ton, rats darting
in the shadows underneath. Sun beat every
thing to dust. The ridge of mountains
where we rode our horses cooled the west;

at night the coyotes sang.

Of the land I have returned to every
year. The first developments parceling
the hills, the reservoir on the river,
the missile plant on the hogback, mall
replacing mall, the country club,
the walled communities, "Columbine,"
"Grant Ranch," "Titan Road," "Bowles
Avenue" where Joseph's field stone house
still sentinels his last ten acres. Water,
open space—Littleton's gold.

The country changes once again.
Not just mine, it is everybody's landscape
now, from Plattsburgh to Littleton, the same,
from this windy Adirondack lake to the river
Platte, the same: the gunfire, the bombs,
the children running, the children falling,
the fear, the disbelief, the closed schools,
the tolling bells, the secluded parents,
the community of grief, the questions,
the fixing of blame, the waiting—the same.
What have we forgotten? What do we expect?
Stone dropped in still water, circles ripple
outward always wider touching everything
until they ring the earth.

Guilt

is a creature burrowed deep
a web of fungus in the soil that bursts

into a horde of mushrooms overnight,
a hundred compromises, a thousand white lies.

You admit your guilt. It brushes near, you
treat it like it's special. Fed, it grows.

You own it, even when it's purged. Bindweed
ripped from the garden faithfully returns.

What's the price of your indulgence? Easy
to let the cat grow fat, bad for his heart

to make the dog suffer because you cannot bear
her loss, to fail your dying mother when you're

not there to hold her hand. And Columbine, like
all the others since, so close, yet safely far away.

Guilt blossoms in a thousand thoughts and prayers.

Fireworks Before the Fourth

Last light on this longest day,
peepers at full throttle.
Already I'm headed toward sleep
when I hear the first bang then
another, not the rapid retort of
a weapon but irregular, as if someone
has paused after each blast to light a fuse.
When did I learn to distinguish
between fireworks and gunfire?

Before I think to expect her
the dog is panting under the bed
rattling the floorboards.

I have not made it to the window
in time to see the bright trail
of sparks, the shower of fire
umbrellas in the night sky.
Startled, I miss the beauty of it.
Somebody's birthday or wedding
perhaps, a celebration of light
and noise that the mountains
answer back, this dazzling
invention from ancient China.
In the Mideast men fire shots
into the air for pure joy.

Crackle of lesser firecrackers,
then silence. I wait, braced.
The night sounds do not return.

It's okay, I tell the dog. Nothing
to fear, unless one considers
how one explosion leads to another,
how pyrotechnics and warfare
sprang from the same womb, how
technology became their handmaid.

That is why the soldier home from battle
clutches the arms of his easy chair;
why tonight I can imagine the sound of gunfire
bouncing off a mountain in Afghanistan.

Deepwater Angel

—After such knowledge, what forgiveness?
T. S. Eliot, *Gerontion*

It was a summer for rabbits.
Nibblers of lettuce, gnawers
of beans, they ate everything
we tried to grow. But in
the morning light they played,
leaping high in the air, twisting,
running, often five at once.
This year, few rabbits, no jumps.
The bats are gone.
Each summer evening they
crawled from a crack
in the roof, over 100 little
brown bats (we counted them)
that swooped for bugs
on webbed wings, killed
by a fungus tracked from cave
to cave by hikers. A dead bat is
no bigger than a silver dollar.
Mosquitoes claim the garden.

Tonight a coyote signals in
a long quavering crescendo
aimed at May's planting moon.
From the woods answering yips—
wow wow wow—like a distant
siren, falling, dying, three, maybe
four in the pack, probably
related. They are suddenly
quiet. When they resume, they
are joined by a barred owl, eight

measured hoots in counterpoint
to the random howls. If the noise
is no comfort, silence is worse.

In Washington blame has reached
a shrill pitch, as if all the howling
and hooting could stop
the hemorrhage.
Oil hangs in giant plumes
from the surface of the sea
fingers its way toward shore,
strokes the barrier reefs,
probes the marshes. Blood
of the world wasted, wasting,
fouling all it touches.

On dark water floats a seabird,
so coated with oil it's difficult
to tell what kind it is. Shiny,
stiff with death, its stretched
wings are still beautiful,
feathers splayed to ascend
the air, to ride skywards
on heaven's bright currents.
What price for tinkering
with this earth?

Deepwater angel, take flight.
May your next world be unknown.

January Freeze

At night the furnace beds down,
clicks a tattoo in the baseboard
as metal contracts. Morning,
with luck, the reverse; warmth
mounts in the walls, pinging gently.
On the night the fuel oil gels
and the furnace quits, not heat
but cold begins its stealthy climb,
slowly at first, not much noticed
just a vacancy, a silence of cold
creeping into rooms, skin, bones,
despite woolens and woodstove.
We crouch above it, rubbing our
hands and thinking of fire,
nothing else, hugging ourselves
while outside the chill sun reigns.

Zero out, the two stray cats huddle
inside a makeshift box on the porch,
chimney smoke stands in pillars against
the sunbright sky, so dry, dust rises
like snow from the road where
tracks from yesterday lie petrified.
The dog on her leash dances from foot
to foot, breath short in this knifing
cold that cuts clean to the core.

At the head of a line of cars mine
sets the pace, unwelcome because
my eyes want to stray to the pasture
where stone-still horses stand, backs
to the sun, to the icy lake devoid

this day of fishermen who endure
the cold like cats, but I know to keep
moving, to focus only on the streak
of gray ahead while I wait for the last
frost to clear from the windshield,
for the pure bright light to filter down
and my own vital heat to rise.

Wake Up

On the radio this morning
they played something truly
remarkable—the sound of unknown

birds around the world awakening
to first light, starting in the east at dawn,
going west—hoots, howls, warbles,

then riffs and trills as another
contingent, another continent woke
up, until I could feel earth itself

turning with its brocade and bristle
of trees and music, that strange
and lovely communion of birds.

I wished and failed to name them.
Miffed, I let other thoughts jump in—
What were they doing? Why were they

singing? For mates, for space, for joy?
I heard only myself, my mind a darting
squirrel making a din, while the dawning

music slowly died. Maybe it's time to listen.
To think sunrise, birds, trees, earthturn.
To sing a little song at daybreak.

About the Author

Alice Wolf Gilborn, a graduate of Wellesley College and the University of Delaware, is the founding editor of the Adirondack literary magazine *Blueline,* now published by the English Department, SUNY Potsdam. She is author of a chapbook, *Taking Root* (Finishing Line Press), as well as two books of nonfiction: *What Do You Do With a Kinkajou?* (Lippincott) and *Out of the Blue* (Potsdam College Press), a winner of the best book of nonfiction from the Adirondack Center for Writing. Her poems have appeared in numerous journals and anthologies, including *The Writer, The Lyric, Blueline, A North Country Quartet, Healing the Divide* and *After Moby-Dick.* In 2012 and 2018, she was lead editor and publisher of two volumes of poems by Vermont poets, *Birchsong: Poetry Centered in Vermont.* She is a member of the Authors Guild, the Poetry Society of Vermont, and is listed in the Poets & Writers Directory.

See her website at: alicewolfgilborn.com for more information and samples of her work.

Artist Mary Schwartz, from East Dorset, Vermont, paints "nature captured through the lustrous medium of egg tempera…. I paint landscapes of Vermont and Delaware, where the quality of light, colors, textures and contours are part of my everyday life….My paintings are meant to portray my life in nature, to evoke the deep feelings I have for its beauty." See www.mschwartzarts.com.

www.ingramcontent.com/pod-product-compliance
Lightning Source LLC
Chambersburg PA
CBHW070335090426
42733CB00012B/2486